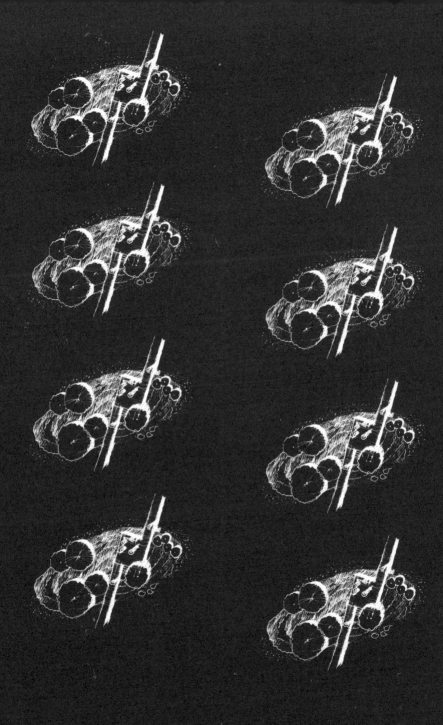

**Nature
Site
Restraint**

ORO
EDITIONS

Publishers of Architecture, Art, and Design
Gordon Goff, Publisher
www.oroeditions.com
info@oroeditions.com

Published by ORO Editions

Text: Annemarie Lund, Udo Weilacher, Marc Treib
and Thorbjörn Andersson
Graphic Design: österling grafisk form & fotografi
Copy Editor: Bonnie Lovell
ORO Project Coordinator: Kirby Anderson

10 9 8 7 6 5 4 3 2 1 First Edition

Library of Congress data available upon request.
World Rights available

ISBN: 978-1-943532-44-5

Color Separations and Printing: ORO Group Ltd.
Printed in China.

International Distribution: www.oroeditions.com/distribution

Nature|Site|Restraint

Thorbjörn Andersson Landscape Architect

Essays by:

Annemarie Lund
Udo Weilacher
Marc Treib

Nature

ANNEMARIE LUND

THE CONCEPT OF NORDIC landscape architecture as underplayed, socially and functionally, while still being beautiful has not only been predominant, but also admired. This consensus is reinforced by the fact that Nordic furniture design, culinary skills, and architecture all ride the same wave. In the decades after World War II, with the economy very limited, Nordic landscape architects held the attitude that landscape architecture should be unobtrusive and unaffected yet still possess quality realized with a high degree of skill. They shunned flamboyance and the overdone. The expression of landscape design at the time was based on a place and its spirit—its *genius loci*—and most often was very green. Since then, the concept of Nordic landscape architecture as underplayed socially and functionally while being nonetheless beautiful has endured.

To a large degree, Nordic landscape architecture remains based on a cherished view of nature. Due to differences in background and social structure, landscape architecture in northern Europe differs from landscape architecture in central and southern Europe—and, quite naturally, from landscape architecture in South America and Asia. But given similar topography and location, why shouldn't Dutch landscape architec-

Vinterviken Culture Park, Thorbjörn Andersson 1998.

ture resemble that of Denmark, or Canadian landscape architecture be similar to that of Sweden, Norway, and Finland? The difference was especially evident in the 1950s and 1960s, and that Nordic difference endures. Is this due to a national soul, the welfare society, or the long, light summer nights?

From the beginning of the 1900s, the landscape profession developed a quite different focus from earlier years, with landscape architects designing fewer private gardens and far more public schemes. Projects typically involved open areas for the numerous suburban housing projects built to mitigate post-World War II housing shortages. Among these were public parks and squares, landscapes for educational institutions, sports facilities, and cemeteries. A tight economy during these postwar decades greatly limited the richness of the schemes, a limitation regarded as positive. Any boastfulness, pomposity, or blustering expression was to be avoided. Creating unpretentious schemes that were functional, beautiful, and served the people was more desirable—this was regarded as a virtue in itself.

I first met Thorbjörn Andersson in the mid-1980s in Malmö at a conference for landscape architect journalists, to which we had both been invited as press representatives. Although he had only recently completed his studies, Thorbjörn had already distinguished himself as a writer focused on investigating the nature of landscape architecture. He wanted to understand the past as well as to examine the contemporary scene, and to present the past as a possible basis for creative activities. Unusual for his age, he was greatly aware of what was happening on both the Nordic and international scenes.

As one of its three founding editors, Thorbjörn was a frequent contributor to the Swedish journal *Utblick Landskap* (Landscape Review), which during its years of publication (1984–2000) presented the landscape art and personalities of the past as well as contemporary landscape architecture. In 1987 and 1990, it produced two issues in collaboration with the Norwegian journal *Byggekunst* and the Danish journal *Landskab*. Among his work as the author or editor of several books, he initiated and co-edited *Svensk trädgårdskonst under fyrahundra år* (Four Hundred Years of Swedish Landscape Design, 2000). This book offered an outstanding and much-needed introduction to Sweden's landscape architecture, including the significant Swedish landscape personalities who have led both practice and education in the second half of the twentieth century.

Being part of a minor language region creates the problem of self-understanding—in this case about landscape architecture—left undiscussed in a larger context; there is thus the risk of becoming fixed and self-reinforcing in one's thinking and practice. In landscape architecture, architecture, and design, Scandinavia is often considered a somewhat homogeneous enclave. This is also true regarding social institutions, the welfare society shared as a common goal, and in terms of language. The landscape foundations in the Nordic countries, however, are actually quite different. The landscape of Denmark, being primarily flat with extensive land devoted to agriculture, differs markedly from the landscape of Sweden and Norway. In contrast to the landscape design tradition of Sweden—at times criticized by Danish landscape architects like C. Th. Sørensen as being too naturalistic—Danish landscape expression has tended to be more apparent.

In general, Danish landscape architects rely more on geometry contrary to their colleagues in other Nordic countries, where landscape design traditions have been enriched by varied starting points. Nordic landscape architecture's near allegiance to nature and cultural landscapes possibly derives from the fact that the urban population previously consisted of relative newcomers from the countryside. Although today most Scandinavians were born in the city, their interest in nature seems to be reviving, perhaps stimulated by the concern for climate change.

Good landscape architecture depends on historical patterns as well as subsequent long-term city planning. For many years, the Nordic countries have displayed a vital concern for the planning of public spaces, obvious in the work of eminent city planners, municipal architects and gardeners, and other professionals who have contributed to the urban fabric of their cities.

This book presents eleven works by landscape architect Thorbjörn Andersson, landscapes in which we see a furthering of the Swedish tradition. To a large degree, each design responds to the given place and emphasizes its inherent spirit. With one exception, all the projects involve squares, parks, cemeteries, and public urban spaces and meeting places whose many seating opportunities encourage social interaction. These parks serve as part of the city and/or the local community, a welcome and necessary "void" in the urban mass. They can be reviewed in the following categories:

Planting based on the cultural landscape. The principal aim of these projects is to enhance the conditions inherent in the site and yet transform them by using the features of the surrounding landscape, such as wooded areas, groves, orchards, and hedges. At the Askim Memorial Grove, near Gothenburg, flowering crab apple and cherry trees mark the arrival of spring, while maple trees broadcast bright autumn colors; each accentuates the course of the seasons. In other works, the reference to the woods or orchard has been stylized. At Hyllie Plaza, the reference, no doubt, is the beech forest of southern Sweden—but used without its woodland understory. Here the forest is re-formed as short, parallel rows of trees set on the plaza's pale granite surface, accompanied by a set of elevated pools that can be seen as a dark forest pond. In a similar manner, the flowering fruit trees arranged in precise rows on the Umeå Town Hall Square mimic the apple orchards of the greater cultural landscape.

Many of Andersson's designs offer special gardens with rich and concentrated profusions of flowers—most evident in the convent-garden-inspired, but newly interpreted, scheme for the Novartis Campus, the "sunken garden" at the Askim Memorial Grove, and in the gray-blue tones of the seaside garden at Dania Park. All three places, one could claim, retrieve the image of the country garden's large perennial beds—dense and well-defined—but here offered as public or semipublic garden spaces.

Terrain. A concern for the natural character of the land has directed even modest movements in the terrain in Andersson's work, with small hills preserved and existing wetlands and ponds carefully regarded. On the Umeå University campus, the hilly green landscape with its clusters of trees reinforces the lake's natural character, in a manner similar to the campus park at the Lund Institute of Technology. This is not to imply that the terrain has been left as it was. In places, the grassed land has been terraced, so that the contour lines are marked by 15- to 20-cm-high risers—similar to the contours of several landscapes by the Finnish architect Alvar Aalto. This treatment is also evident at the Borås Textile Fashion Center, in Sandgrund Park, and in the Askim Memorial Grove. In Andersson's landscapes, the terrain is rarely left completely flat, in contrast to the absolutely horizontal floors of the neighboring buildings; these areas of reshaped terrain create many fine experiences for the visitor. More evident, perhaps, is the surface sloping toward the water at Sjövik Square: a unique experience.

Spatial sequence. Rarely are spaces marked by symmetry or evident geometry: instead, spaces usually flow as a freer sequence, an aspect of the design difficult to imagine from its plan. That is to say, the influence of the terrain on the landscape must typically be experienced on site. Sandgrund Park is shaped as a long, curved space with five lozenge-shaped ridges. In its hollows, groves of beech and magnolia trace the "tongue" of the land.

Borrowed landscape. Strong and precisely formed elements—such as viewpoints, steps, bridges, decks, and terraces—provide a counter to the natural and designed landscapes. Especially effective are the vantage points Andersson provides on wharfs and piers, features that strengthen the opportunities to "borrow" the landscape. These vantage points often provide the possibility for freeing oneself from the limits of the immediate area by offering a clear view of features beyond the boundaries of the site.

This design tactic was first evident at Dania Park, where the large raised wooden bastion in the northwestern corner encourages visitors to look out over the strait—a feature also used by youngsters to jump into the water. In a similar fashion, both sides of the Sandgrund Park peninsula provide viewing platforms that accompany a shoreline boardwalk that terminates in an additional platform. In a similar way, a terraced wooden deck at Sjövik Square leads visitors closer to the water, while a pier on the opposite side of the square lifts them out over the water while simultaneously providing a view across Årstaviken toward the Tantolunden park. Likewise, Panorama Terrace in Rinkeby elevates the visitor above the surrounding buildings and opens an almost infinite view over the expansive, coarse natural landscape. By employing the Japanese tradition of "borrowing" the surrounding landscape, Andersson enriches the given scheme by providing more and ever-changing views. The use of this device suggests that the joy of nature and its lushness are deeply rooted in the Swedish national soul.

I am fully aware that design approaches such as a flowing spatial sequence, "borrowed" landscape, varied treatment of the terrain, and planting based on cultural landscapes are frequently employed in many landscape designs, but in Andersson's work, they take different forms that depend on the specific conditions of the place. The art of moderation colors his working method, treatment of form, and choice of materials. That Thorbjörn Andersson's schemes give a contemporary expression to old virtues reveals a deep-rootedness in the nature of Sweden and a respect for its people.

References

Andersson, Sven-Ingvar, and Steen Høyer. *C. Th. Sørensen—Landscape Modernist*, Copenhagen: The Danish Architectural Press, 2001.

Andersson, Thorbjörn, Tove Jonstoij, and Kjell Lundquist. *Svensk trädgårdskonst under fyrahundra år*, Stockholm: Byggförlaget, 2000.

Kassler, Elizabeth B. *Modern Gardens in the Landscape*, New York: Museum of Modern Art, 1964.

Landskab, a Nordic magazine for landscape architecture, landscape planning, and urbanism that provides historical documentation of Nordic landscape architecture. *Landskab* began in 1920 as *Havekunst*; from 1969–1980 it was titled *Landskap*. Issues dated 1920–2016 can be downloaded from www.landskabsarkitekter.dk/tidsskrift/.

Shepheard, Peter. *Modern Gardens*, London: Architectural Press, 1953.

Treib, Marc, Tom Simons, and Alexander Ståhle. *Places, Platser: Thorbjörn Andersson, landskapsarkitekt*, Stockholm: Svensk Byggtjänst, 2002.

Utblick Landskap, the Swedish journal for landscape architecture and gardening, published 1984–2000

Translated from Danish by Pete Avondoglio.

Site

UDO WEILACHER

Whether people are fully conscious of this or not, they actually derive countenance and sustenance from the "atmosphere" of the things they live in or with. They are rooted in them just as a plant is in the soil in which it is planted.

Frank Lloyd Wright, 1954.[1]

ACCORDING TO ECONOMISTS, we are now in the third phase of a digital evolution that started in 1991, the date of the first upload of a website to the World Wide Web.[2] Today's world is deeply rooted in digital technology that creates specific atmospheres and colors all human perception of landscape and nature. Therefore, it is impossible to discuss the development of landscape architecture in the last decades, especially the relationship between people and site, without considering global digitalization.

The influence of digitalization on landscape architecture ranges from the major changes to human perception caused by globally disseminated stereotypical landscape images to the sophisticated digital technology in landscape design offices that promises a more accurate comprehension of complex natural systems. Huge amounts of digital data have been collected, often by satellites and drones. In *Flights of Imagination: Aviation, Landscape, Design,* landscape historian Sonja Dümpelmann points out that "Flight, in particular powered flight, which first developed in the early twentieth century, has changed our perspectives of the world, has transformed our perceptions and imaginations of the world, and has changed the landscape itself and the ways we design and inhabit it."[3] The increasing use of drones is accelerating this development, particularly since small remote-controlled quadcopters equipped with digital cameras are affordable by a broad audience. Far more advanced drone technology is used to generate huge 3D point clouds, georeferenced and connected to large relational databases. Experts consider this the beginning of a completely new dimension and approach to landscape, allowing "for considerable progress in matters of landscape modeling and representation. Point Cloud Technology has become central to most methods of design and analysis, and is used regularly to produce elaborate sections, elevations, and plans from the remote sensing data."[4]

But does digital high-tech equipment really help landscape architects better understand their field of operation, a certain site? Or is this just the technologically fired prolongation of a long-lasting, most likely unwinnable, chase of an ancient demon—the demon of total environmental control? Evidence gathered in the last three decades suggests that technological progress rarely leads to a more profound comprehension of a site. Without question, a remote-controlled drone view from above facilitates a distanced, scrutinizing observation of landscape, but it does not necessarily lead to greater comprehension of the hidden layers and deeper meaning of the environment, both of which can be achieved only by carefully listening to the site. The digital approach to landscape is perfectly in sync with contemporary society's continued quest for a technological way out of an environmental crisis generated by this very same technology.

Given this background, the traditional Scandinavian approach to landscape might seem anachronistic—but precisely because of that, it is possibly more valuable than ever before. "Historically, in Scandinavia there has been a deep trust in nature and nature's methods that formed the basis of national cultures, including urban cultures," Thorbjörn Andersson explains. "This has to do with a landscape tradition that includes comparatively late urbanism, and a comfort found in nature and nature's values, which form a sort of moral context: nature as supplier of simplicity, directness and logical solutions, seems to be the inherent belief. Even more important is that nature provides authenticity [...]. Authenticity is one of the few ways to discuss our need for reality."[5]

Since it is impossible in the Age of Humans to clearly differentiate between natural and artificial environmental components, the thesis that "nature" can provide authenticity is questionable.[6] But "authenticity" is also associated with the personal bodily experience of space, an emotional approach rather than a rational examination or purely economical evaluation of an environment.[7] The digital evolution that has taken place in recent decades has not supported authenticity and has instead led to an increasing rupture between people and their living environments, sometimes described as a loss of place attachment. "Place attachment implies 'anchoring' of emotions in the object of attachment, feeling of belonging, willingness to stay close, and wish to return when away."[8]

Scandinavian landscape design in general, and Thorbjörn Andersson's approach in particular, is very successful in anchoring emotions to designed open spaces. This is achieved with formal austerity, clarity of lines, and a sparing and specific use of plants and building materials—but also from a successful blending of an artistic approach to design with one social and scientific. Most important is a profound feeling for the atmosphere of the Swedish landscape, said to be influenced by the "northern light." "Here in the North the sun does not rise to the zenith but grazes things obliquely and dissolves in an interplay of light and shadow. [...] Nordic light thus creates a space of moods. In the North we occupy a world of moods."[9] Unusual in the digital age, Andersson is proficient in the art of "listening" to the site: "The existing site provides valuable input that can be used in the course of design. This information, however, is often embedded, hidden—and ambiguous. To interpret the site, a profound understanding of the greater landscape is required. To attend to the inherent qualities of a site means dealing with the characteristics of the site but also with how they can be used."[10]

Spaces designed by landscape architects have to fulfill daily functions in the "man-made system of spaces superimposed on the face of the land," but they also must offer sensual experiences and inspiration.[11] Landscapes designed by Thorbjörn Andersson are impregnated with differentiated atmospheres that underline the character of specific sites and strengthen the attachment to place. His projects give people the opportunity to bodily experience the site and become rooted in its atmosphere. Phenomena that cannot be perceived haptically—especially light, air, space, and movement—contribute to five characteristics of his work that define a site's atmosphere.

1. The essence of vegetation. Vegetation is decisive for the character of a space. Even a single tree can create space while strongly accentuating the quality of the local atmosphere. The size of a tree, the girth of its trunk and the structure of its bark, the anatomy of its branches and twigs, the volume and density of its canopy, and the texture and coloring of its leaves—all these are key characteristics. The position of the tree is also important, whether planted as part of a row or group, or whether it remains solitary. The distance between the planting, its harmony with the architectural surroundings, and many other aspects are also significant. Trees reduce air temperature while rendering the movement of the air visible and audible. They produce a unique aural carpet. Their swaying in the wind contributes to visible movement within the space. According to the season and the time of day, trees, shrubs, and perennials offer accents of color and traces of scent through their flowers, fruits, and leaves. Through them, the course of time can be experienced. "We know that light filtering through a leafy tree is very pleasant—it lends excitement, cheerfulness, gaiety; and we know that areas of uniform lighting create dull and uninteresting spaces."[12] Since natural daylight continually changes, so too does the atmosphere of a landscape. At night, artificial lighting shapes the site, often significantly changing the appearance of the vegetation and character of gardens, parks, or plazas. In projects by Thorbjörn Andersson, artificial lighting always underlines the specific character of a given site; his tree plantings are never arbitrary, but always specific.

2. *The movement of topography.* Hardly any other attribute determines the character of a site more strongly than topography. Geological and other natural forces like wind, water, and ice have shaped an infinite variety of ground formations on the earth's surface, which in the most literal sense are of fundamental importance for a landscape's character. Topography has an impact on all settlement forms and affects the growth of vegetation and the local climate. Topographic design interventions always change the face of a landscape and have far-reaching consequences for the *genius loci,* the total character of a site. Topography not only forms a landscape but also circumscribes it, gives it shape and structure, defines its scale and dimensions. Topography frames the experience of light and air, different on an exposed hilltop than in a sheltered valley. Topography makes people sense movement physically—it is energy made visible.

The Swedish landscape, especially along the rugged, rocky coastlines, openly shows its topographical characteristics, inviting the landscape architect to react sensitively with respect for the spirit of place.

3. *The liveliness of water.* As a life-giving and lively medium, water is of central importance for a site's atmosphere. Water, whether liquid or solid, is abundant in Swedish landscapes: it reinforces the colors of moistened surfaces, affects the ambient temperature, and underlines by its flow dynamics the topographic characteristics of a place. Reflective, still water surfaces such as ponds and lakes bring light into the landscape and radiate calm, but they also show the movement of air when the slightest breath of wind creates gentle ripples on the water. Waterfalls, fountains, and bubbling creeks produce liveliness in parks and gardens. On the seashores of Sweden, the unrestrained and often-changing temperament of the sea shapes the atmosphere and brings movement. Water provides sound qualities in a space—rushing, splashing, gurgling, bubbling—and gives the air near the sea an unmistakable taste, or a special scent when summer rains start to fall on the dry land. Through water, people perceive light, air, the space, and its sound. And it makes movement in landscape capable of being experienced sensually.

4. *The accord of materials.* Thorbjörn Andersson shows great passion and joy in his work with the different materials naturally existing on-site. He understands how materials react with one another, how they sound, how they are brought to a shine, and what weight and presence they have in a space. Since almost all materials appeal to the senses, they influence the emotional experience of light, air, space, and movement. Pavements absorb or reflect light; they get hot and heat up the ambient air or remain relatively cool, even in full sunlight. Materials have an effect on the colors of a space, making it appear

hard or soft depending on whether stone, wood, or metal is used for walls, decks, pergolas, and so on. Quiet spaces do not tolerate an excessive variety of materials. Whether a surface consists of natural stone, asphalt, or concrete slabs, whether it is water-bound or gravelled, pavements and coverings condition the sound of a space in many different ways. They influence pedestrians to slow down or speed up, making their movement audible. Materials determine the palpable surfaces of a space and make contact with a space pleasant; they invite people to play boules or attract skaters; materials are loud or quiet, colorful or homogeneous.

5. *The invitation to stay.* At times, designers clutter public spaces with art objects and furniture, perhaps fearing that the site might look dreary or empty, especially when not in use. Public design becomes especially disturbing if too many single objects in a space compete as the focus of perception. With too many competing elements, the sensory experience of the landscape becomes disrupted rather than encouraged. Experienced landscape designers understand that overfurnishing is more likely to harm the character of a site than simplicity. The simple park bench set at the right place, the picnic table at the edge of a clearing, the small kiosk at the waterfront, and similar elements that invite people to stay and experience the site are typical in projects by Thorbjörn Andersson.

Even if all five components are combined in a design and form a whole filled with character, it should not be forgotten that any designed space is always embedded within a particular context. No open space exists isolated from its surroundings; listening to the site also means carefully listening to the context. Parks border on city districts or landscapes; gardens adjoin houses, other gardens, or streets—these in turn are part of a road network; plazas are generally enclosed by buildings of different functions, sizes, and styles. For determining the character of a site, the atmosphere of the context is decisive. It is obvious that human activities contribute to the atmosphere of a landscape as well. Whereas these activities can be influenced by design to a certain extent, the moods and feelings of people are beyond the control of landscape architects. So in the end, the atmosphere of a place remains to a great extent indeterminable and ineffable, not least because of ever-changing weather conditions. To create a comfortable atmosphere, and to give people the chance to become truly "rooted" and "anchored," listening to the site and experiencing it physically are more important today than ever before.

Notes

1. Frank Lloyd Wright, *The Natural House,* New York: Horizon Press, 1954, p. 112.
2. See Claudia Lemke and Walter Brenner, *Einführung in die Wirtschaftsinformatik, Band 1: Verstehen des Digitalen Zeitalters*, Berlin: Springer Gabler, 2015.
3. Sonja Dümpelmann, *Flights of Imagination: Aviation, Landscape, Design*, Charlottesville: University of Virginia Press, 2014.
4. Prof. Christophe Girot, https://girot.arch.ethz.ch/research/point-cloud-research-in-landscape-architecture, accessed 7 March 2019.
5. Thorbjörn Andersson, "Scandinavia: Reduction, Response, Authenticity," in *Territories: Contemporary European Landscape Design,* ed. Joseph Disponzio, Cambridge, MA: Harvard University Graduate School of Design, 2007, p. 107.
6. Elizabeth Kolbert, "Enter the Anthropocene–Age of Man," *National Geographic,* 2 March 2011, pp. 60–85.
7. Deriving from the Greek word *authentikós,* meaning "original, primary, at first hand,"
8. Maria Lewicka, "In Search of Roots: Memory as Enabler of Place Attachment," in *Place Attachment: Advances in Theory, Methods and Applications,* ed. Lynne C. Manzo and Patrick Devine-Wright, New York: Routledge, 2013, p. 49.
9. Christian Norberg–Schulz, *Nightlands: Nordic Building.* Boston: MIT Press, 1996, pp. 1–2.
10. Thorbjörn Andersson, *10 Notions About Landscape Architecture*, Stockholm, 2015, n.p.
11. "A landscape is not a natural feature of the environment but a synthetic space, a man-made system of spaces superimposed on the face of the land," J. B. Jackson, *Discovering the Vernacular Landscape*, New Haven, CT: Yale University Press, 1984, p. 8.
12. Christopher Alexander, Sara Ishikawa, and Murray Silverstein, *A Pattern Language: Towns, Buildings, Construction*, New York: Oxford University Press, 1977, p. 1106.

Restraint

MARC TREIB

SCIENTISTS HAVE OFTEN characterized natural processes as embodying an "economy of means": the production of maximum effects using minimal amounts of material or energy. That same description might also apply to most of the landscapes designed by Thorbjörn Andersson over a thirty-year professional career. In lectures, Andersson has frequently cited his interest in a small early-nineteenth-century book by the poet and social critic Carl Jonas Love Almqvist, whose title translates as *The Significance of Swedish Poverty*.[1] In his text Almqvist asserts that the nation's moral fiber and material culture derive from its being "poor"—a term he uses metaphorically to describe Sweden's demanding environmental conditions, restricted varieties of natural resources, and, at the time of his writing, limited technology and human lifespan. In terms of landscape practice, an acceptance of "poverty" would imply that one begins by addressing the limitations placed upon a project by site, climate, technology, and budget, thereafter treating these restrictions as positive factors. While in some instances, true poverty did trouble the lives of a segment of the Swedish people, in most cases—and in the Andersson landscape—the term should be regarded as a synonym for simplicity, modesty, or restraint.

As in the Nordic countries, "poverty" has also characterized the design culture of Japan, a system of values that extended from its crafts to its landscape design. If Sweden has been constrained by climatic severity and granite bedrock, Japan has been shaped by heat, humidity, earthquakes, limited amounts of arable land—and from the seventeenth century until the start of the modern period, governance by sumptuary laws. Japanese designers confronted these restrictions by crafting forms and formulating spatial ideas rooted in simplicity. The aesthetic of "refined poverty," for example, governed the making of the utensils, architecture, and gardens of the tea ceremony, where the making of virtually every aspect of the tea environment reflected reduction and refinement.[2] Of course, Andersson works in a time where, in contrast to the past, resources and technologies are readily available for realizing landscape architecture. Many of his projects, in fact, have enjoyed funding sufficient to support the use of excellent materials. Yet despite the wealth of options available to him, he has often chosen to pursue a modest design rather than one marked by complexity and extravagance.

Although lacking the same concern for refinement as the material culture of tea, the *Arte Povera* ("poor art") movement based in 1960s Italy also represented a conscious return to the use of unremarkable materials. Often simply arranged, *Arte Povera* sculptures and installations represented a willful rejection of evident composition and prior aesthetic determination. What intrigued Germano Celant, the curator most closely associated with *Arte Povera*, was "the discovery, the exposition, the insurrection of the magic and marvelous values of nature" embodied in these works.[3] Order and composition derived from situation and process. Being in the quotidian world, however, landscape architecture must address a far broader range of concerns than those governing art within or outside the gallery. Landscape architects can nonetheless carefully investigate the conditions that underlie the project and use only simple means to fashion a "poor" landscape. Although modest and insightful interventions were already characteristic of Andersson's early projects, the thinking and values behind them did not derive directly from his academic education. In the 1980s, the years Andersson was at university, Swedish landscape education regarded design as subservient to concerns for ecological performance and social accommodation. Although disappointed by this reduced attention to the actual making of landscapes, he nonetheless appreciated learning about ecology and environmental processes. After graduation Andersson traveled widely through parts of the world, unusual for a Swedish landscape student at that time. Among those destinations was the San Francisco Bay Area, where he spent about a year studying, working, and learning from the region's landmark modern landscapes. If this exposure to new ideas in a new land was one formative influence, so too was his native landscape heritage. Throughout the centuries, whether those more historical or those closer in time, "making do" with what you have and keeping things simple remained the governing values shaping Swedish landscape architecture. In the twentieth century, the landscapes of Erik Glemme and Gunnar Asplund stood out among those who had profited from these values.

Limits provide starting points; limits are accepted; limits must be overcome. Early Andersson projects were modest in their assertiveness, understandable given his youth, the nature of the commissions, and at times the budget at hand. The conversion of the former Nobel dynamite works to a park in Stockholm's Vinterviken (1999, see p. 4) and the remaking of the 1840s Hamnparken in Jönköping (2001) both relied on the simple device of low retaining walls to restructure the terrain into a field of stepped terraces—in all, simple reformations of the earlier topography. In Jönköping, ribbons of granite wall weave through the existing trees, retaining the soil while providing elongated linear surfaces for seating. In an almost Japanese manner, this gesture alone brought the existing landscape and contemporary use into greater accord.

Over time, his commissions grew in scale, the breakthrough project being Dania Park in Malmö, whose construction in 2001 accompanied the conversion of derelict harbor land into a new residential quarter—a trend already common in postindustrial cities worldwide. As its name implies, the park faces Denmark, whose low topographic profile is visible across the Öresund on clear days. The task facing the landscape architect was to create park space destined primarily for passive recreation, although some active play would be permitted on the park's central lawn. As the park's design, success, and subsequent popularity have been documented in numerous publications, they need not be repeated here. But it is worth noting that Dania Park deftly mixed an address of its social use with innovative formal investigation and did not remain a schematic diagram charting interpersonal activities. For example, along the park's shoreline, attached to a series of enclosed seating pods, are stepped viewing terraces that reach out to the sea. These units articulate the promenade that terminates in a sizable social area crowned by a narrow "gangplank" thrusting outward over the water.

With the completion and popularity of Dania Park, numerous commissions followed, commissions that have included several more parks—whether renovated, converted, or newly constructed—plazas, and improvements to the campuses of educational institutions. Almost all these works have used relatively restrained means to transform landscape. Certain of these projects might rightfully be termed "interventions," although each addition—how- ever small—has also been critical for reshaping the greater landscape as well as the immediate site.

One landscape type recurring in Andersson's practice has been the design or redesign of the central plazas of cities with relatively small populations, or districts of populous cities such as Stockholm and Malmö. Sjövik Square (2010) in south Stockholm pioneered an approach shared with several of the plazas that followed. The generating intention was to create a vibrant public space that joined land and sea—rendering both areas more active and the link between them more accessible. As in most Andersson designs, the scheme was nuanced and enriched by more than a single idea. Two rows of trees frame the square, soften the impact of the neighboring apartment blocks, and direct the view outward toward the water. Benches, a playground, and wooden surfaces for taking the sun in appropriate weather accommodate the square's social functions. The large boulders that dot the plaza are frequently commandeered as seating and performance stages by teenagers and children.[4] At first glance, the linear pool near the lower boundary of the square appears redundant—after all, the sea itself lies just beyond the walk that separates them. In contrast to the depth and potential danger of the sea, however, the shallow basin allows younger children to delight in wading and splashing in its water.

The more recent Town Hall Square in the northern Swedish city of Umeå (2018) followed a similar schema, using double rows of red maples (*Acer rubrum*) along its east and west edges to define a central space, while simultaneously effecting a transition to the dense urban fabric around it. A small grove of crab apple trees at the square's northwest corner—which flowers brilliant white in spring—provides a zone of greater intimacy. The center of the square is left relatively neutral, enlivened only by an argyle pattern of Swedish granite set before the town hall. As a somewhat neutral space, it accommodates a variety of activities called for in the original program as well as those that arise spontaneously. In all, the plaza is neat and simple—almost classical in its governing order, yet modern in defining its constituent zones. Although some visitors might read the design of the Umeå Town Hall Square as too simple, I suspect Swedes might be more apt to call it *snygg*, that is to say, "handsome," "tidy," or "trim." But perhaps that characterization is really just another demonstration of what can be achieved using only restrained means.

An element that appears in several Andersson landscapes, whether for the city, the shore, or the campus, is a wooden deck given various shapes, sizes, and siting. In some ways, these platforms all descend from the gangplank first poised as the concluding moment of Dania Park. In a related way, at Sandgrund Park in Karlstad (2008), the narrow wooden wedge that cantilevers dramatically over the Klar River concludes visitor movement through a terrain of elegantly graded grassed mounds. In other landscapes, the wooden deck takes form as a promenade, a terrace that brings people to the water, or supports views across the water or over the land. At the Umeå University campus (2010) and at the technical institute in Lund (2016), wooden decks attract students to their respective ponds by enfolding linear walkways with areas of greater measure designed specifically to accommodate students in groups and to foster their social interaction. The wooden terrace/decks are arranged at two elevations: the upper level offers students a more complete overview of the water and surroundings; the stairs and decks on the lower level deliver students to the edge of the water. The materials in both landscapes are common, restricted to wood and metal; the detailing is straightforward yet refined. Like a stage set in theater, the decks support use in a somewhat neutral way, rather than attracting attention to themselves. As a result, the landscape architecture serves as a "delivery system" for joining students with land, water, or vegetation.

Poverty and restraint might also suggest the reliance on only a single species of tree, for example, the selection of native beech as the principal element of Hyllie Plaza in Malmö (2010). Here the European beech (*Fagus sylvatica*) was selected for its ubiquity in the southern Swedish landscape, although it should be noted that its use in urban conditions presented considerable technical challenges. The beeches are configured in rows that divide the plaza's spaces into slices that terminate in an open zone fronting the sports arena. Here an aligned series of elevated water channels energizes the plaza and guides visitors to their sports or entertainment venue. At night, strings of lamps overhead, supported by light standards of colossal dimensions, conjure a sense of an artificial sky. Beech trees, granite surfaces, troughs of water—in all, quite restrained means.

Not all Andersson's projects are so restricted in species, materials, or forms; others have profited from more lavish funding or a more forgiving climate. But of his complete body of work, I regard as most significant those landscapes marked by restraint—"poverty," if you will—interventions that have developed more from the appropriation of what already existed than from what has been renovated or added. Like the adept use of punctuation marks by a skilled author, the well-placed insertion or supplement—or at times removal—has sufficed to bring the landscape and its new uses into accord.

Everyone, especially those in the design fields, must exercise value judgments when allocating resources at the personal, local, regional, and national levels. Italian artists created works they conceived as "poor art." The Japanese elevated "poor" design to an art form, and some of the country's greatest art—including garden design—has been marked by reduction and the judicious shaping or placement of commonly available materials. Limits often generate creativity.

A "poor" approach has not been restricted to the design professions, however. In the 1960s, the Polish dramaturge Jerzy Grotowski (1933–1999) formulated what he termed a "poor theater." Grotowski felt that true theater, effective theater, derives not from sensational staging that requires massive amounts of resources but from the mental state of the actors and their ability to effectively communicate that state to the audience—so as to solicit their appropriate reaction. In some ways, Grotowski's approach marked a return to the very origins of drama, traveling backward in time past the Greeks to a theater using neither masks, music, costumes, nor elaborate lighting: in all, a raw theater.[5] This is not to say that Andersson attempts or achieves similar extremes; to the contrary, certain recent projects display a richness of materials and details. But I do believe that despite any surfeit of features or materials, behind almost all his landscape designs lie a certain modesty and consequent restraint, and a wish to put what is at hand to their best uses, those appropriate to the site, and those appropriate for the intended audience. Perhaps Grotowski's poor theater is actually closer in means and feeling to the "poor" Swedish world described by Almqvist centuries ago. Both share the basic idea that it is substance rather than materials, artificiality, or flash that characterizes the significant work, whether in theater, art, building—or landscape architecture.

Notes

1. Carl Jonas Love Almqvist, *Svenska fattigdomens betydelse*, 1838, reprint, Hedemora: Gidlund, 1989.

2. See Kakuzo Okakura, *The Book of Tea*, 1906, reprint, Rutland VT: Tuttle, 1989.

3. Germano Celant, *Arte Povera*, New York: Frederick Praeger, 1969, p. 225.

4. Part of *A Time Machine on the Square* by Jan Svenungsson whose inscriptions are based on recent newspaper headlines.

5. Owen Daly, "Source Material on Jerzy Grotowski: Statement of Principles,"19 June 2004, https://owendaly.com/jeff/grotows2.htm, accessed 22 December 2018.

Projects

Dania Park, Malmö

DANIA PARK (Daniaparken) is located along the water's edge of the Öresund strait that divides Sweden and Denmark. Before development the site had been a flat and barren landfill: an industrial desert of contaminated mud. Landscape qualities on the existing site were hard to identify but eventually positive aspects of a more ephemeral kind became evident: the light, horizon, long views, sky, wind, and sea. It is a place to experience weather and seasons. Those qualities served as the point of departure for the design. The immense scale of the coastal landscape is reflected in the elements of the park and their spatial disposition. The park's principal features are the Scouts: three inclined concrete planes that intersect the rough boulder shoreline and permit park visitors to reach the sea. The Bastion, a 40 × 40-meter flat table elevated some six meters above the sea, leaves the visitor exposed to the elements, whether a harsh wind or a beautiful sunset. The Balconies—three large wooden trays—overlook the large, slightly sunken grass meadow called the Lawn, which is protected from sea winds by a double row of Swedish whitebeam trees (*Sorbus intermedia*) and salt-resistant shrubs (*Rosa* and *Elaeagnus*).

All the features in the park turn to the sea; all activities orient toward the water. The majestic coastal landscape, adjacent more than distant, is made part of the park experience. In the design, the greater landscape has been visually borrowed into the park to celebrate the sea.

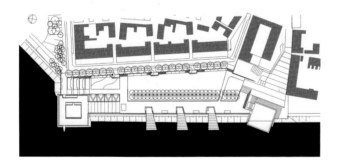

Dania Park, Malmö, Sweden
Design team: PeGe Hillinge, Veronika Borg,
Anders Lidström, Sven Hedlund, Peter Ekroth,
Clotte Frank, Michael Hallbert (lighting)
Area: 20,000 square meters
Opened: 2001

Sandgrund Park, Karlstad

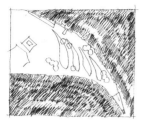

AT ONE POINT in its length, the Klar River that runs through the city of Karlstad splits to form a 300-meter-long cape; from the air it appears as the pointed beak of a bird. The cape is a powerful landscape, a place of considerable drama, and the site of Sandgrund Park (Sandgrundsparken).

For many years before the park's construction, the area had been fairly desolate, without a sense of destination. The river was an obvious feature to address in the design process, as well as the cape, whose pointed tip terminates in the water. Those same qualities are reinforced and amplified in the design of the park. A system of boardwalks along the river's edge extends into the water, welcomes the sunset, and stresses its proximity to the water. The tip of the cape was given a more architectural profile, reshaped into a 40-meter-long viewing platform. The ground was modeled as an undulating terrain of five parallel ridges, the first measuring six meters in height, the remaining mounds given gradually lower profiles. Their elevated crests offer green viewpoints along the ridges; in contrast, the valleys between them provide containment. Every other valley harbors a distinct plant habitat, among them a beech forest, a magnolia grove, and a fern valley.

The aim of the Sandgrund Park design has been to transform an anonymous sandbank into a place of significance, a place in which, and from which, to enjoy the grandeur of the surrounding river landscape. It is a place to gaze at the river and enjoy its flow and reflections through the variations of all four seasons.

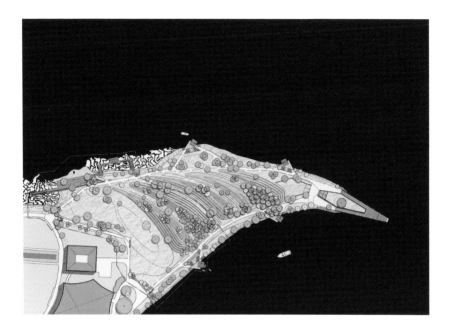

Sandgrund Park, Karlstad, Sweden
Design team: Johan Krikström, Jimmy Norrman,
Emma Norrman, Lisa Hellberg, Margareta Diedrichs,
PeGe Hillinge, Lennart Knutsson (construction),
Helena Björnberg (lighting)
Area: 40,000 square meters
Opened: 2008

Hyllie Plaza, Malmö

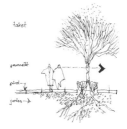

NO TREE IS MORE characteristic of Scania, Sweden's southernmost province, than the beech—and no other species bears such a strong association with its native region. The horizontal branch structure that supports its canopy, paired with the equally horizontal orientation of its leaves, produces a quality that is almost architectural.

The competition entry for the new Hyllie Plaza (Hyllie Torg), located in a southern district of Malmö, bore the motto *Fagus*, the scientific name for beech. The idea driving the design was to establish a beech forest on the plaza, or better stated, to form the plaza as a beech forest. However, the beech does not thrive in the conditions provided by the site and to ensure the survival of the trees would require help. In response, significant biological research began, an effort that included the contributions of a team of experts trying to find a high-tech solution for ensuring the life of the beech grove. The first necessity was a gigantic planting bed whose dimensions equalled those of the plaza above it. This earthen layer consisted of an 80-cm-thick base of structural soil, of which voids comprised 60 percent to guarantee sufficient oxygen. This planting bed was capped with Swedish high-density granite paving totalling 12,000 square meters in area. Into this granite field, twelve parallel trenches were cut, each planted with lines of beech trees. By their placement on the plaza, the trees form a series of glades.

To provide night-time illumination, eleven tall masts were grouped as pairs along the sides of the plaza. Between these masts stretch 1,800 meters of steel cables. The cables support a field of 2,800 LED diodes programmed to conjure four seasonal scenarios that create a digital sky after dark.

51

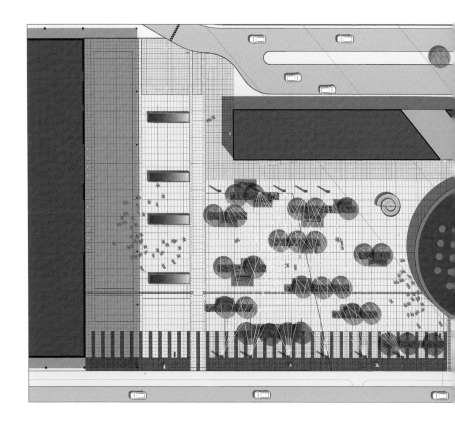

Hyllie Plaza, Malmö, Sweden
Design team: Johan Krikström, Marianne Randers,
PeGe Hillinge, Niklas Ödmann (lighting),
Örjan Stål (soil construction)
Area: 14,000 square meters
Opened: 2011

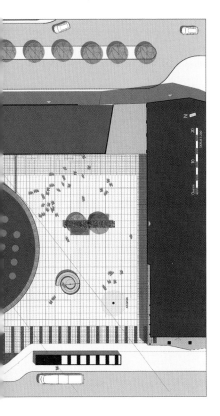

Campus Park, Umeå

UMEÅ UNIVERSITY is a young institution, founded only in the late 1960s. Here, about 35,000 students from all over the world study subjects in a broad range of disciplines. Located on the coast of the Gulf of Bothnia in the far north of Sweden, the campus stands only some 300 kilometers south of the Arctic Circle.

A campus park should offer its students a variety of places that encourage informal discussions and the free exchange of ideas. In contrast to the University's enclosed lecture halls, classrooms, and laboratories, open nonhierarchical spaces such as these support the creative interaction among students, researchers, and teachers that is critical to learning. The quality of the campus park thus supports the attractiveness and the academic activity of the University in both its educational and social programs.

Campus Park at Umeå University consists of 23,000 square meters of sun decks, jetties, open lawns, walking trails, and terraces, all organized around a constructed lake. Within the lake, its principal island extends as a small archipelago with bridges that lead to the southern shore. Here the visitor meets a hilly landscape with sunny as well as shaded vales, articulated by the white trunks of birch trees. In front of the student union a lively outdoor lounge—a series of gravelled, fan-shaped terraces—orients to the sun. Each terrace is shaded by multi-trunked trees and furnished with tables and chairs that support a variety of uses.

CAMPUS PARK UMEÅ

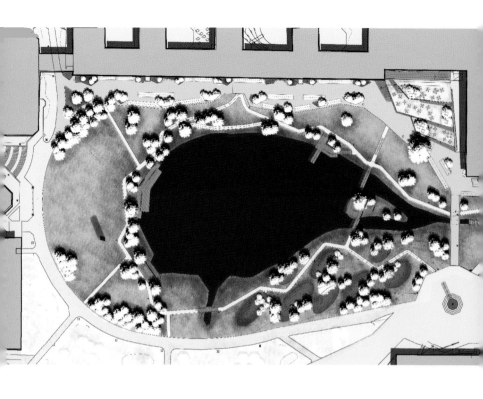

Campus Park, Umeå University, Sweden
Design team: Staffan Sundström, Emma Norrman,
Mikael Johansson, Alexander Cederroth (lighting)
Area: 23,000 square meters
Opened: 2010

Sjövik Square, Stockholm

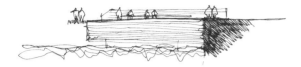

STOCKHOLM, A CITY ON THE WATER, is set at the
convergence of two archipelagoes: the fresh-water Lake
Mälaren stands on one side; the salt-water Baltic Sea on
the other. A mosaic of convex rocky islands occupies the
space between the two. These islands and water shape the
essential geographic qualities of the Swedish capital.
The design of Sjövik Square (Sjövikstorget) draws on
these properties. Situated on the Årstadal quay, the square
opens toward the water and the greater landscape. To re-
inforce this basic intention, the square takes form as a soft-
ly sloping plane angled toward water and the view.
A pair of hundred-meter-long wooden promenades
frames the plaza and brackets the view. Along their outer
edges, surfaces for sitting encourage contact with the social
life of the plaza. A pier hovering above the water extends
forty meters beyond the quay at the plaza's eastern limit.
Included in the design is a 35-meter-wide water feature: its thin curtain of water, popular with children,
rushes over a surface sheathed with Norwegian slate.
Partly integrated in the water is a sculpture by the artist
Jan Svenungsson. This artwork consists of three very large
boulders, one engraved with headlines drawn from Stockholm newspapers' front pages commemorating the date
the boulder was placed.
To borrow a distant landscape aided by a framed view is
a classic technique used in Japanese gardens. It is a logical
practice: at times the strongest features of a site actually
may lie beyond its immediate borders. This is also true for
Sjövik Square, where what lies within its boundaries joins
with what lies beyond.

Sjövik Square, Årstadal, Stockholm, Sweden
Design team: PeGe Hillinge, Jimmy Norrman, Emma
Norrman, Lin Wiklund, Helena Björnberg (lighting),
Jan Svenungsson (sculpture)
Area: 12,000 square meters
Opened: 2010

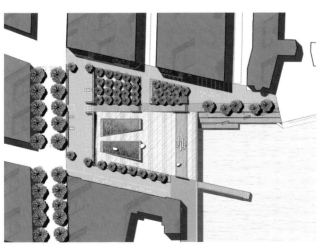

SJÖVIK SQUARE

Novartis Physic Garden, Basel

FOR ALMOST TWO DECADES the Novartis pharmaceutical company has undertaken a major building program to create a research campus graced by buildings and landscapes of extraordinarily high-quality design. One of the campus blocks, designated as a space for common use, hosts the Physic Garden, which features plants significant to the development of the pharmaceutical industry. In that sense, the Physic Garden can be said to represent the core of the company's activities. Its design relates to the medieval monastic garden in which monks developed knowledge about the pharmaceutical substances found in plants, knowledge that laid the foundation for today's research efforts.

The garden is organized as a theater, with a backdrop of yew (*Taxus*) and hornbeam (*Carpinus*) hedges of different heights that draw the visitor forward. At its center is a sunken planting bed organized as a series of stripes that contains thirty-two of the most important pharmaceutical plants. Viewed from above, the bed reads as a colorful and textured painting or carpet. Bridges of light construction span the sunken bed and permit visitors to more closely examine the plants, each of which is labeled with an engraved bronze bar mounted at the edge of the bed.

Four "log racks," each a collection of timber stacked in piles, frame the sunken bed and complement in form the screens of hedges. The types of wood represent species from which chemical substances have been extracted and used in the pharmaceutical industry. Amphora-like drinking fountains provide water for visitors and grant the garden another dimension. All in all, eighty-three plant species are on display in the Physic Garden.

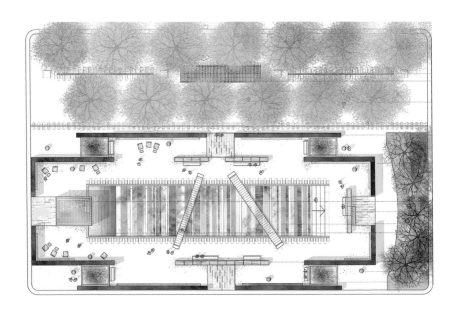

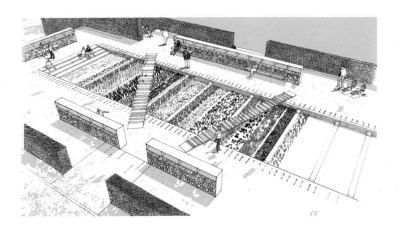

Novartis Physic Garden, Basel, Switzerland
Design team: PeGe Hillinge, Johan Krikström,
Johnny Lindeberg, Emma Norrman (plants),
Therese Egnor Rezine (plants), Pål Svensson
(fountain sculptures), Alexander Cederroth (light),
Markus Moström (graphic design)
Consultants: Schönholzer + Stauffer GmbH, Ernst
Basler + Partner (structural engineering)
Area: 2,800 square meters
Opened: 2012

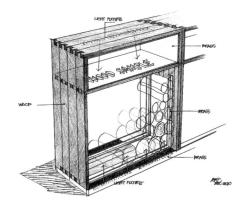

Textile Fashion Center, Borås

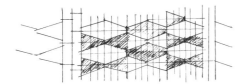

IN FRONT OF THE ENTRANCE of the recently-opened Textile Fashion Center, which houses the Swedish School of Textiles, lies a carpet of stone, 110 meters long and eleven meters wide. The pattern of the carpet was inspired by a method for weaving complex patterns introduced in 1805 by J. M. Jacquard, its design thus representing the legacy of textile production. Constructed using three different types of granite, this linear plaza serves as the primary public space for the school, programmed with various activities to ensure a lively social life for students, faculty, and staff.

The City of Borås is considered the heart of the Swedish textile industry. The Textile Fashion Center, known locally as Simonsland, hosts educational programs for textile designers as well as a museum devoted to the subject. Since 2014 these activities have been situated in an assembly of old factory buildings that date from the 1870s. In the life of the students, the outdoor areas play an important role. The students' primary social interaction takes place here, as do informal meetings, seminars, and the free-flowing discussions important for a rich academic life. Simonsland offers many such spaces, spaces marked by different qualities: shaded, sunny, bustling, or intimate. The River Viskan runs through the campus, offering an opportunity to experience, or even engage with water.

In the agglomerated dense campus area, separate outdoor rooms are found. Complementing the entrance zone with its granite carpet is a shaded, almost mystical, space having the river as its floor, and suspended walkways hugging the building façades around it. Further along, a new pedestrian bridge with a see-through floor links the two banks of the river.

Textile Fashion Center, Borås, Sweden
Design Team: PeGe Hillinge, Staffan Sundström,
Ronny Brox, Per Johansson and Johan Lidström (lighting)
Consultants: DTH Arkitekter, with Sweco Architects,
Stiba (construction).
Area: 40,000 square meters
Opened: 2014

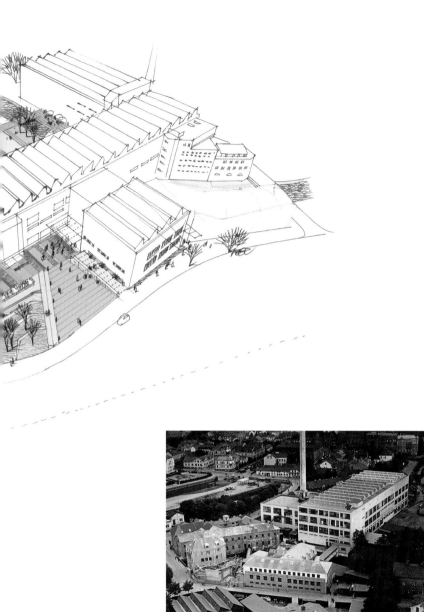

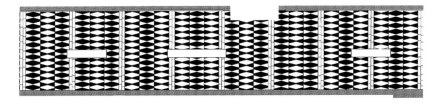

Pond Park at LTH, Lund

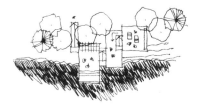

THE CAMPUS of the Lund Institute of Technology (Lunds Tekniska Högskola, or LTH) occupies a large site, once farmland, that slopes gently to the east. The University was established here in 1961 to provide advanced learning and technical faculties, including architecture, in the Swedish south. Today the LTH offers higher education for 10,000 students. The original architect for the campus was Klas Anshelm, who laid out what is today a dozen buildings: simple, solitary red-brick volumes, independently sprinkled across the slope. The result is a handsome, if barren, campus with little to join the faculties or provide amenities for its students.

The project for the Pond Park addresses these shortcomings by establishing focal points clustered around the two ponds—remnants of a clay quarry long defunct—that occupy the center of the windswept site. These former clay pits are today deep shafts cut in the ground filled with water. Compared to the flat surfaces of the surroundings, this is dramatic terrain. The slopes descending from their rims are steep, in places almost vertical. The generating concept for the new landscape was to render the steep edges of the ponds accessible in differing ways, with new construction to create socially attractive places and promenades. The western rim of the larger pond offers places to sit, enjoy the view, and meet with friends and colleagues. Sundecks and platforms are located high above the water, close to the rim of the depressions containing the ponds. The concept for the east side of the pond differs markedly. A winding promenade creates smaller social spaces, while a system of stairways moves up and down along the drop, in some places reaching all the way down to the water.

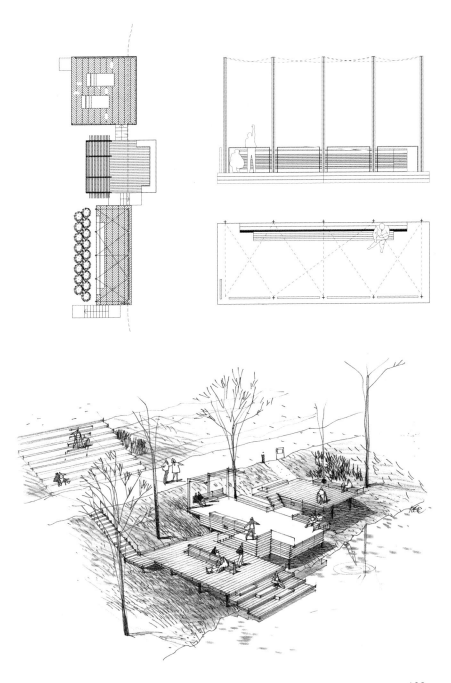

POND PARK LTH LUND

Pond Park at LTH, Lund, Sweden
Design team: PeGe Hillinge, Staffan Sundström,
Nicholas Bunker, Monica Zuniga (lighting)
Area: 17,000 square meters
Opened: 2016

Askim Memorial Grove, Gothenburg

A MEMORIAL GROVE is a place for those who have been left behind to remember those who have departed—a refuge for those in search of consolation, reflection, and the memories of loved ones. It is an asylum, a vehicle to support the bereaved in the difficult times after the loss of a relative or friend.

When the parish of Askim, in southern Gothenburg, planned to extend its burial grounds, it was decided that the new section should be designed as a memorial grove rather than a zone for traditional earth burial. The old cemetery and the church, which date from 1879, share the crest of a hill; the extension of the cemetery is shaped as a smooth bowl with grass terraces placed on the adjacent lower level. The focal point of the bowl—a shallow pond with still water—reflects the sky above, while a paved ceremonial terrace provides an earthbound communal setting for candles and flowers. In places the memorial grove is planted with trees selected for their seasonal change: species such as crab apple, flowering cherry, and maple, graced by brilliant autumn color. The rustic granite wall that encircles the site provides a sense of enclosure and ensures a quiet atmosphere that enhances private reflection.

A memorial grove should create a place inviting and beautiful, metaphorically serving as the meeting point between the living and the dead. It should be a haven which speaks to us, a place where we recall memories of those we miss. A memorial grove serves an important mission in modern society. It should tell us that even if life is hard today, there is the possibility of a brighter tomorrow. It is a harbor not ultimately for the dead, but for those who remain.

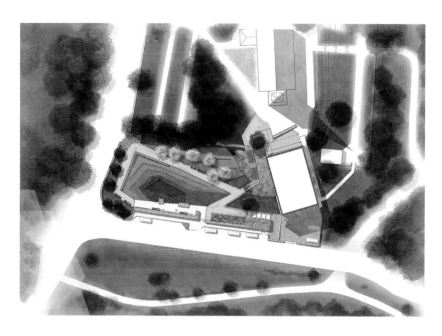

Askim Memorial Grove, Gothenburg, Sweden
Design team: Staffan Sundström, Charlotta Löfstedt,
Tobias Phersson, Peter Erséus, Malin Unger
Area: 3,500 square meters
Opened: 2017

Rinkeby Panorama Terrace, Stockholm

RINKEBY PANORAMA TERRACE is a viewing platform overlooking Järva Field, a large recreational area for a socioeconomically vulnerable population living in northern Stockholm. The architectural environment in Rinkeby is typical of the 1970s, the era in which the district was developed, marked by industrially produced housing and poor-quality public space. To the north a four-lane highway separates central Rinkeby from Järva Field. In 2007, a political vision led to efforts to improve the social and environmental quality of the municipality. These efforts included burying the highway in a tunnel and reestablishing a comfortable connection between the new housing areas on top of the tunnel and the large recreational field below.

The Panorama Terrace occupies a dramatic position on the site and is linked to the field by a sloping promenade, named *Pendenten* after the Italian term for a slope. The viewing platform on the crest of the terrace is designed to resemble a large wooden lamp. The eight-meter-high angled walls are constructed of planks with spaces between them that emit the light generated within. The promenade is planted with Russian olives (*Elaeagnus angustifolia*) and articulated by eight stone sculptures, carefully positioned in the landscape.

The project aimed to create a place of high experiential quality and to connect Rinkeby with the adjacent suburbs, a strategy intended to increase social integration. This is one of those instances when landscape architecture makes a political and social difference.

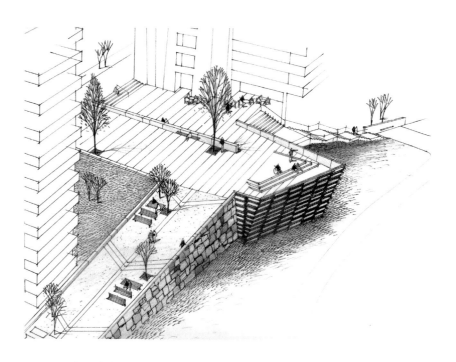

Rinkeby Panorama Terrace, Stockholm, Sweden
Design team: PeGe Hillinge, Anna Norén, Joel Berring,
Fredrik Toller, Catrin Jonsson, Frederik Schönfeldt,
Ronny Brox, Alexander Cederroth (lighting),
Marco Cueva (sculpture)
Area: 4,000 square meters
Opened: 2017

Town Hall Square, Umeå

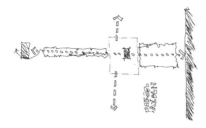

TOWN HALL SQUARE (Rådhustorget) in Umeå provides a
stately setting for the Town Hall, a red-brick building in the
Dutch Renaissance style that dates from 1888—it stands
as the center point of the largest city in northern Sweden.
The new square plays a major role in the structuring of the
city's public space, pairing the carefully considered use of
trees with a simply paved central area. An allée of maples
(*Acer rubrum*) running along the square's east side ends at
a low glazed pavilion with indoor as well as outdoor café
service, oriented optimally to maximize the beneficial
effects of the sun. The allée to the west, in turn, finishes
with a crab apple grove (*Malus* "Everest") that blooms as
a spectacular mass of white in May. The canopies of these
trees hover over a set of shallow canals that resembles a
system of irrigation channels. Six stone amphorae, an artwork by sculptor Pål Svensson, are the source of the water.
The paving in the central part of the square is laid out as a
carpet, with a pattern inspired from a local weaving technique using two colors of granite. This part of the square is
purposely kept open to hold events of different kinds that
vary with the seasons. In the winter, a labyrinth of snow
occupies the space. In summer, visitors may encounter an
occasional outdoor cinema, market, or some other sponta-
neous event. Movable chairs offer informal seating. They
are all marked with the birch leaf, the symbol of Umeå.
Because of Umeå's location at 65 degrees north latitude,
any landscape design for the city must acknowledge seasonal change, for example: a lighting program especially
created for the dark winter months.

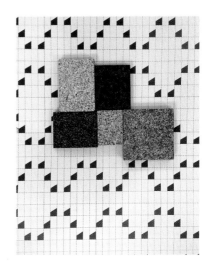

Town Hall Square, Umeå, Sweden
Design team: PeGe Hillinge, Tobias Phersson,
Fredrik Schönfeldt, Niklas Ödmann (lighting),
Pål Svensson (sculpture)
Area: 9,000 square meters
Opened: 2018

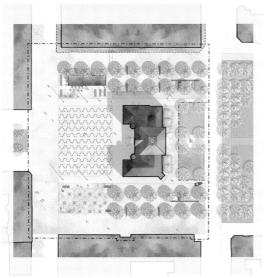

Credits

Thorbjörn Andersson has practiced landscape architecture since 1981, having studied landscape architecture, architecture, and art history in Sweden and the United States. His work reveals a continued focus on the design of public spaces in the city and their relation to the society they serve. A selection of these projects, which have received international attention and various awards, were previously published in the book *Places, Platser* (Svensk Byggtjänst, 2002).

Andersson has authored or co-authored numerous essays, contributed chapters to books in Sweden and abroad, and served as a founding editor of the Swedish landscape journal *Utblick Landskap*. An elected member of the Royal Swedish Academy of Fine Arts, he is currently Professor of Landscape Architecture at the Swedish University of Agricultural Sciences in Ultuna, in addition to his continuing professional practice. His teaching experience includes visiting professorships at several schools internationally. For his contribution to the field of landscape architecture, in 2009, Thorbjörn Andersson was awarded the Prince Eugene Medal from His Majesty, the King of Sweden.

Contributors

Annemarie Lund is a landscape architect, author, critic, and former adjunct professor at the University of Copenhagen. For three decades she served as editor of *Landskab*, the Danish journal of landscape architecture.

Udo Weilacher is Professor of Landscape Architecture and Industrial Landscapes and department chair at the Technische Universität of Munich (TUM) and the author of several books and numerous articles about landscape architecture and art in Europe.

Marc Treib is Professor of Architecture Emeritus at the University of California, Berkeley, and a landscape and architectural historian and critic who has published widely on modern and historical subjects in the United States, Japan, and Scandinavia.

Acknowledgments

The projects published here have been planned, designed, and implemented by various design teams at Sweco Architects, Stockholm, under the leadership of Thorbjörn Andersson. The majority of these have been conceptualized in collaboration with architect PeGe Hillinge.

Financial support for this book has been received by the Royal Swedish Academy of Fine Arts, the Stockholm Building Society and the Helge Ax:son Johnson Foundation.

Photo credits

Linnea Svensson Arbab: 37 Kasper Dudzik: 46, 52–53, 54, 55, 57, 77, 105, 108, 112–113 Anna Rut Fridholm: 75 Patrik Lindell: 38–39, 74, 76, 78–79 Jens Markus Lindhe: 33 (bottom) Åke E:son Lindman: 4, 31, 34–35, 36, 41, 42, 44–45, 47, 48–49, 50, 58–59, 61, 68–69, 93, 100–101, 102, 103, 106–107, 110, 111, 114, 116, 117, 118–119, 121, 122–123, 125, 126, 128–129, 131, 132–133, 138–139, 141 Mikael Lundgren: 135, 142–143 Jens Raeber: 82–83 Beat Rösch: 90 Scanpix: 33 (top) Nils-Olof Sjödén: 96–97, 98 August Wiklund: 140

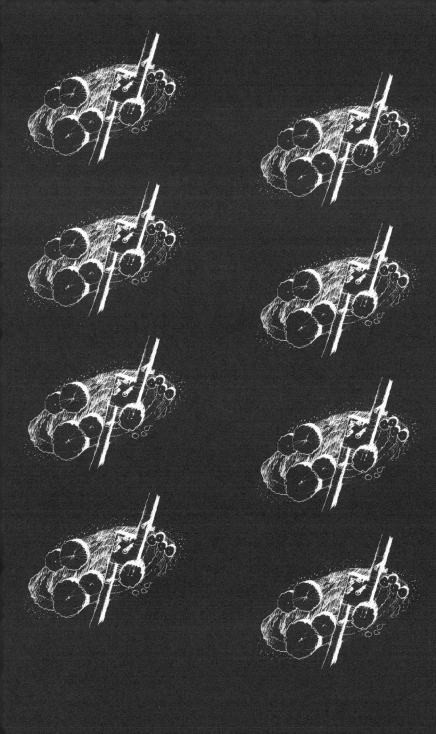

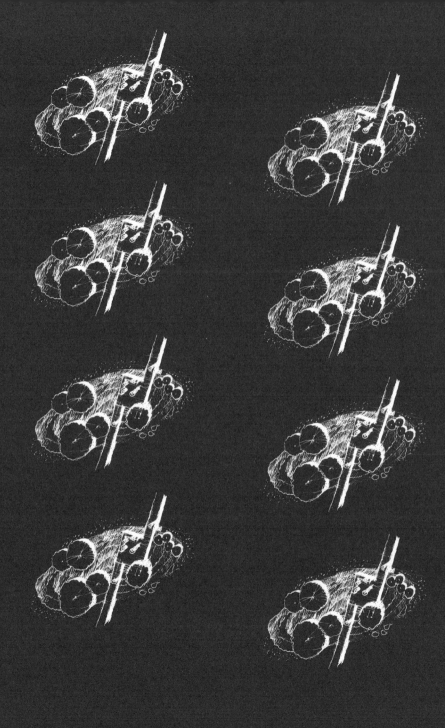